WORK RIGHT

✔ Straight-Talk Strategies
for
Personal and Professional
SUCCESS

STEVE VENTURA

CONTENTS

Results

INTRODUCTION

Cutbacks. Reorganizations. Hiring Freezes. Having to do more … with less.

You read it in the paper. You hear it on the evening news. Maybe it's touched you, personally. It certainly is no secret. In one way or another, many people today are facing some tough economic times. And that goes double for the organizations we rely on to supply the jobs we need – and the paychecks that allow us to provide for the people we care most about.

What's your situation? Are you working? Has your business been able to stay IN business? If so, congratulations – you're one of the lucky ones. But, unless you're blessed with unlimited good fortune, luck alone won't keep you employed. And over the long haul, it alone won't bring the success your organization needs to survive, thrive, and offer continued work for you and your colleagues.

So if luck isn't the best strategy, what is? How can you not only enhance your job performance but also continue building a satisfying career? What do YOU need to do? The answer is: You have to WORK RIGHT! And that involves mastering "The 3 R's" – a different 3 R's than those you learned as a child … **"The 3 R's" of workplace success:**

Respect

Responsibility

Results

Respect includes how you view, treat, and deal with other people – and how you present and conduct yourself (how you *behave*) – on a daily basis. Responsibility entails doing your part, taking your job seriously, meeting the expectations that come with your paycheck, and being a dependable person of integrity. **Results** is about getting things done … about making a positive contribution to your organization and its mission. All three of those components are critical to your workplace success. And all three are what this handbook is all about!

On the pages that follow, you'll find **twenty-four "to do's"** – a collection of ideas, mindsets, and proven strategies guaranteed to help you perform better in your job and enhance the relationships you enjoy with your co-workers. They're written in a real-world, "pull no punches" style, so get ready for some straight talk – the kind we *all* need to hear and remember.

As I've said in previous works, pay attention to what you're about to read. You owe that to *your organization* – the one that not only hired, trained, and pays you, but also has entrusted you with its resources, its mission, and its future. You owe it to *your fellow team members* – those whose welfare, performance, job security, and successes are inextricably linked to yours. Most importantly, you owe it to YOURSELF – the one who must live with the image you see in the mirror … the one who ultimately benefits from, or is hurt by, the actions you take and the employment track record you add to each day.

USE and APPLY the information in this handbook, and you'll not only improve your overall effectiveness, but you'll also build a reputation (and a legacy) as a top-notch contributor – someone who …

WORKS RIGHT!

The most important

single ingredient in

the formula of success

is knowing how to

get along with people.

~ Theodore Roosevelt ~

MASTERING "THE 3 R's"

Respect

Respect for ourselves guides our morals;
respect for others guides our manners.

~ Laurence Sterne ~

Extend an Ear

Listen to Others

Don't you just hate it when people don't listen to you ... when they won't extend the common courtesy of looking you in the eye and making an effort to hear (and understand) what you have to say? The messages they're sending: Your thoughts, ideas, and opinions (YOU) aren't all that valuable; their agenda is much more important than anything you might have to say. That's inconsiderate. That's rude. That's DISRESPECTFUL. And, if you're looking to maintain positive, productive relationships with your coworkers, it's something you need to avoid doing yourself.

Fact is, you earn the right to expect others to listen to you by listening to *them*. So, whenever someone comes to you with an idea, a concern, or just something to share, take the time – *make* the time – to give them a few minutes of your attention. And if you really are too busy to stop what you're doing even for a minute or two, schedule a time when you *can* get together and chat.

Any exceptions? Any times when you ought NOT to listen? Yes there are! If someone is badmouthing the business, or spreading rumors and gossip, or telling discriminatory/off-color jokes, you should tactfully suggest that doing so is inappropriate – and then walk away. To do otherwise is to con- done that behavior. And that makes you as wrong as the person doing it. The good news: those are *exceptions*. Most of the time, people have valu- able things to say. Like you, they are good, positive people who deserve the respect of being listened to.

Ever catch yourself thinking "Nobody listens around here"? If so, make sure you're not one of those nobodies!

Dignify Differences

Respect Diverse Cultures, Ethnicities, Backgrounds, and Ideas

If you had to identify behaviors that are counterproductive to being successful at work – things to *avoid* doing ... reputation and career killers – what would be on your list? Look close to the top of mine and you'll find the following: Believing that (and behaving as if) one is an elite member of the "chosen few" – that only those just like you are right and correct ... that your way is the *only* way.

The misguided souls (I'm being really kind with that label) who fall in this behavioral category are fairly consistent in their thinking. People from different cultures? *Foreigners!* Members of different age groups? *Fogies or punks!* Coworkers with different work ethics? *Lazy or "brown nosers"!* Those with different ideas? *Whackos!* Individuals of different color? *Second-class citizens (or much worse)!* The common theme running through their Cro-Magnon brains: Different (from me) is wrong. And that's a mindset that just won't cut it in today's multi-demographical workplaces. To borrow a line from my book *Start Right ... Stay Right*, it's time for those who embrace that philosophy to unscrew the top of their heads, throw out some of the garbage in there, and catch up with the human race!

Look around your organization. Focus on the people. What do you see? Chances are there's a mix of different backgrounds, ages, and ethnicities. Some are "like" you – some aren't. But each of them has a part to play in keeping your business strong. Each has a contribution to make. Like you, each of them is important and unique. Each brings something special – something *different* – "to the table." And like you, each deserves respect (and appreciation) for who they are and where they came from.

Here's the deal: My kids are different, my friends are different, my family members are all different, and in some ways, my wife and I are very different. Sound familiar? Clearly, no two people are exactly the same. So if being "different" equated to being wrong, guess what – *everyone* would be wrong … including ME! And that's just not the case.

With few exceptions, different is NOT wrong, it's just different. And the more we accept and appreciate that fact, the more respectful and successful we all will be. Each of us has a choice – we can criticize and berate differences, or we can embrace and celebrate them. Either way, they're not going away. And whichever choice we make says a lot about us – as coworkers and as human beings.

THINK ABOUT IT …

Imagine that four people are having a conversation (in English).
One speaks with an Irish brogue.
One has a Spanish accent.
One speaks with a Texas drawl.
One is clearly from Massachusetts.

Which one talks funny … which one is "right"?

Concentrate on Courtesy

Be Considerate

 Y OU MAKE THE CALL. Who do you suppose is more likely to be successful at work (and in life) – a "me first" person who acts as if he or she is the only person in the world, or someone who is polite and thinks of others as well as him/herself? That *should* be a no-brainer!

Although their numbers seem to be dwindling at an accelerated pace, there are still plenty of nice, considerate people in today's workplaces. Hopefully, you're one of them. They're easy to spot … they're joys to work with. And they tend to have a distinctive vocabulary that mirrors the way they think and act. They regularly use words like:

Please … Thank You!
Let me get that for you … You go first.
What do you think? … How can I help?
I'll turn down my music so it doesn't disturb you.
I made that mess – I'll clean it up!

Considerate people perform "random acts of kindness" on a regular basis. They understand that the best way to serve oneself is to serve others. And, they honor the loved ones who taught them to *always mind your manners* by doing just that.

There *are* those, out there, who feel they just don't have the time to be considerate. To them, I say: **Make the time!** And yes, some people think that being considerate is corny and passé. My reply to them? **Hogwash!** But to all those who do think of others as well as themselves, I say: **Keep it up!** It will serve you and your career very well.

Perform with Pride

Respect Yourself

Here's one you can take to the bank: Everything you do at work bears your personal signature. Each action you take – the way you complete every task, assignment, project, or job duty – is a reflection of YOU. And that fact leads to two questions you'd be wise to ponder and be concerned with:

> 1. What does my personal signature look like?
> 2. Does it portray someone who exhibits pride in him/herself?

Take a moment and think about the people you feel are truly successful at work. Pick a couple of them ... picture them in your mind. Now, answer those same questions (above) as they apply to your success role models. Are these people who cut corners, just do the bare minimum to get by, and couldn't give a flip about quality? Of course not! They are folks who CARE. They care about their coworkers; they care about their customers; they care about their jobs and organizations. Most importantly, they care about THEMSELVES! They understand that **respect** is not something just to be given to others. We must have it for ourselves as well.

Sign your name (your signature) in the box below.

Now look at it ... stare at it ... think about it. What does that signature stand for? What kind of work does it represent? What professional reputation comes with it? Make it meaningful – because it *is* attached to everything you do.

Without self-respect there can be no genuine success.
Success won at the cost of self-respect is not success –
for what shall it profit a man if he gains
the whole world and loses his own self-respect.
~ B. C. Forbes ~

The willingness to accept responsibility for one's own life
is the source from which self-respect springs.
~ Joan Didion ~

Respect your efforts, respect yourself. Self-respect
leads to self-discipline. When you have both
firmly under your belt, that's real power.
~ Clint Eastwood ~

Respect yourself and others will respect you.
~ Confucius ~

A strong, positive self-image is the best
possible preparation for success.
~ Dr. Joyce Brothers ~

I am a big believer in the "mirror test." All that matters
is if you can look in the mirror and honestly tell
the person you see there, that you've done your best.
~ John McKay ~

Make "The Mission" Matter

Respect the Organization's Purpose and Your Part in It

Every business has a "mission" … each organization exists for a specific and primary purpose. And no, that purpose is not just to provide employment for folks like you and me – although that certainly is a positive byproduct that we all count on in order to support ourselves and the people we hold dear.

So, what's *your* organization's mission? Undoubtedly it has something to do with providing goods or services to customers. And your job exists to help make that happen. If there was no connection between what you do and your business's mission, you wouldn't have a job. It's that simple. And you don't have to be a brain surgeon to understand that the more you're in sync with – and contribute to – that mission, the more successful you're going to be. That's just plain common sense.

But as the old saying goes, *common sense ain't always so common* – which is why you occasionally run into employees who think their corporate mission statement is a bunch of management's words in a frame rather than quidelines for them to follow. Oh well, those poor souls are to be pitied. The longer they think and act that way, the longer they'll remain on a career path to NOWHERE!

Here's a little self-evaluation for you – you'll need a pencil and a piece of paper. At the very top of the paper, briefly describe your organization's mission (what you're all there to do). Then, list all of the activities you performed on your last day of work. Finally, rate yourself in terms of how well you performed those activities – and how much you contributed to that important mission. Well, how'd you do?

Hopefully, you did well. And maybe you'd like to do even better. Here are three WORK RIGHT strategies that will help ensure that continued success is in your future:

1. **Know the Mission**
   Understand your business purpose. Be thoroughly familiar with what your organization says it is about.

2. **Share the Mission**
   Believe in your business purpose. Adopt it as a personal value – one for which you offer or accept no compromise.

3. **Support the Mission**
   Contribute to your business purpose. As you begin each task or activity, ask yourself: "How can I do this *in a way that* will further our mission and help bring it to life?" Once you have that answered, the only thing left to do is DO IT!

Share the Spotlight

Acknowledge Others' Contributions

It's pretty much a universal disdain. Nobody likes spotlight hogs who take all the glory at other people's expense – except for the hogs doing it! And even *they* don't like it when the shoe is on the other foot.

You know the type: the ones who – when receiving kudos for a job well done – conveniently neglect to mention that you (and others) were also involved and contributed. And sometimes, your contribution was much greater than theirs – another fact that seems to slip their minds as they proudly accept praise from some well-intended, yet clueless, big kahuna.

Why do they do it? Maybe they're insecure. Perhaps they're trying to balance a scorecard of past screwups. Or it could be they were just born with overactive, inflated egos. There must be a reason. But you know what? I DON'T CARE! Their behavior is still wrong, inconsiderate, and disrespectful. And for those of us that find such behavior unacceptable, it's absolutely imperative that we avoid the hypocrisy of doing it ourselves.

Truth is, we all want to be noticed and appreciated. That's why one of the best ways to build solid workplace relationships is to share the spotlight. So, the next time you're praised for something, don't forget to mention and thank all of your coworkers who had a piece of the action. Make sure you're not the only winner, and others will return the favor.

Think you somehow lose points by making it known that your success was a team effort? Think again! In reality, you gain points … a lot of them.

Behaviors to avoid ...

Top 10 Ways to Destroy Workplace Relationships and Diminish Your Professional Success

1. Looking the other way when a coworker is in a bind and needs help.

2. Assuming you know what others are thinking and feeling.

3. Ignoring (or discounting) others' inputs, ideas, and concerns.

4. Spreading gossip or rumors about teammates.

5. Telling (or condoning by listening to) derogatory jokes.

6. Assuming others are motivated by the same things as you.

7. Hoarding or monopolizing equipment, resources, and information.

8. Blaming others for your shortcomings and mistakes.

9. Criticizing or belittling coworkers in front of others.

10. Interrupting when someone is speaking; finishing their sentences.

    Bonus way ...

11. Goofing off and letting others pick up the slack.

Get Going "Green"

Respect and Protect Resources

Remember the old days when it seemed that the only people who were concerned with protecting resources were either a small collection of conservationists or "tree-hugging, nature-loving hippies with flowers in their hair"? No more. Most of the world has finally caught up with a fact that those pioneers understood from the get go: our natural resources are NOT limitless. Going "green" – respecting, conserving, and protecting resources of all types – has become the *in thing* to do. It's wise. It's prudent. It's cost effective. It's a good business practice. And if you're looking to enhance your professional success, it's a program you need to get on board with. (And yes, I know, I ended yet another sentence with a preposition).

Here's the way it works: If you're going to be an important, valued member of your organization, you have to be a steward of its important and valued resources. That means cutting waste and maximizing usage. It means thinking before you act – considering the impact your actions will have *before* implementing those actions. And it means doing a lot of little things that collectively add up to a critical mass that can make a positive difference for your working environment and your organization's "bottom line" (not to mention our planet).

Where's the best place to start? In your head – by accepting the notion that all resources are precious and should be used wisely. And when it comes to your business – by thinking like a true stakeholder and adopting the mindset (behaving as if) the costs of utilities, materials, supplies, etc., were all coming directly out of *your* pocket.

So how does all that translate into specific behaviors? What can you actually DO to help your organization and therefore your career? Here are a few suggestions. Put a mark next to the ones you're already doing – and keep doing them! For all those you didn't mark, pick a couple and start working to make them daily habits.

- Turn off lights and equipment that aren't needed or aren't required for safety purposes.
- Recycle paper, plastic, glass, aluminum, etc.
- Take and use only the supplies/materials you really need.
- Return unused supplies/materials to the shelf (or inventory).
- Use business supplies/materials for business purposes only.
- Be diligent with preventative maintenance on equipment and machinery.
- Avoid letting water run unnecessarily.
- Keep a/c set comfortably – but not like a "meat locker."
- Keep doors and windows closed when a/c is running.
- Print only the number of documents you actually need.
- Use ceramic coffee mugs instead of foam or paper cups.
- If you do purchasing, shop for the best prices.
- Dispose of toxic/hazardous material in the specified manner.
- Be careful what you pour into sinks and down drains.

Remember that "going green" is not just about eco-friendly activities. It also includes protecting and conserving your business resources as well. Imagine what could happen if everyone in your organization committed to reducing waste by just 10%. Do the math. The results could be extraordinary ... and so could the success you enjoy for doing it.

Slip into
Someone Else's Shoes

Practice Empathy

Ever notice how easy it is to make negative judgments about other people? Whether it's "idiots" we encounter on the road … or "slower than slow" people who serve us … or "losers" who can't play sports nearly as well as *our* kids can – many of us have developed the knee-jerk habit of assigning degrading labels to people we don't know. Nope, we don't really know them, or their situations, or their challenges. But we sure as heck know what they should do. Or at least that's the way it seems when we spout out phrases that begin with: ***They oughta … Why don't they just … It's easy. All they need to do is ….*** We don't know them, but we know what they are; we don't know their situations, but we know what they should do. Hmmmm. If all that seems illogical, unfair, presumptuous, and disrespectful to you, YOU ARE RIGHT!

To be sure, situations involving other people – including those where you work – can seem clear, simple, and very black and white from where you stand. But you need to remember two things: 1) Unless you're dealing with the <u>exact</u> same circumstances, you're on the outside looking in, and 2) The real world is rarely black and white – it's usually shades of gray.

You (we all) need to remember those things, and you need to *apply* them. That requires less presuming and more understanding. It's about making an effort to see things through the other person's eyes … about walking awhile in his or her shoes. And that is called EMPATHY – a critical component of working right.

MASTERING
"THE 3 R's"

Responsibility

We need to restore the full meaning of that
old word, DUTY. It is the other side of rights.

~ Pearl S. Buck ~

Shoulder Your Share

Do Your Part as a Team Player

Unless you happen to be one of those rare individuals who works completely alone (having no interaction with other employees), you *are* part of a team. And regardless of whether your teammates do the exact same job as you, or perform supportive, complimentary tasks, two things are for sure:

1. You all have roles to play in order to get the job done, and
2. Everyone must do their part in order for the team (collectively *and* individually) to be successful.

Without question, the key characteristic of any team is **interdependence.** Everyone *needs* each other … everyone *relies* on each other. The senior manager relies on the HR rep to handle the mechanics of hiring and staffing; the salesperson relies on the tech support staff to keep the computers running; the janitor relies on the purchasing agent to keep cleaning supplies and materials on the shelf. If one person on the team drops the ball, others are impacted – they can't do their work effectively, and far too often, they have to do more than their fair share to compensate for the slacking member who let the team down.

Ever been in the "I have to pick up the slack for someone else" position? If so, you know firsthand how frustrating and disruptive it can be. And you understand, as well as anyone, why it's NOT a situation to create for others. That's something all of us need to remember if we're ever tempted to kick back and shirk our job responsibilities.

Speaking of remembering …

I'm reminded of a guy I used to work with, many years ago, who was an avid sports fan – and an equally avid goof-off at work. He would come in, talk about the previous night's games, rip apart some of the athletes for not being "team players," and then go about his business of doing very *little* business. I remember thinking: how ironical … how hypocritical … how unfortunate for the rest of us on the team. The good news is that our misfortune didn't last all that long. "Time wounds all heels" – and his poor work habits caught up with him. I have no idea where he's working now – or if he has ever realized the error of his ways. But at least he gave me something to write about!

Are you a team player at work? Do you give your best effort regardless of the role you play? Are you dependable? Reliable? Can you be counted on to carry your share of the load? If your answers are all "yes," greater success is definitely in your future. If your answers were "no" or "not really," I wish you good luck wherever you'll be working next. Hopefully that won't be with me.

Nothing will work unless you do.

~ Maya Angelou ~

It was 1980. America was in the
midst of an oil crisis, a hostage crisis, and
a cold war when a rag-tag group of
college kids were challenged to accomplish
what was seemingly impossible.

Their opponents were bigger, stronger, and
more experienced – the best in the world.
Man for man, none of the collegians could
match up against such powerful adversaries.
Their chances were slim; their advantages
were none. They had but one thing going
for themselves: they were a TEAM.
Each player did his part; each could be counted
on to meet the responsibilities of his position.
And as it turns out, that was all they needed.

The "kids" of this story were the members
of the U.S. ice hockey team who – with the
world watching – beat the Soviets at the
Olympic Games in Lake Placid, New York,
and prompted broadcaster Al Michaels'
now famous question:

"Do you believe in miracles? Yes!"

Earn Your Expectations

Be a Role Model

If you're like most folks, you expect a lot from the people in your life – whether they be family members, friends, business associates, fellow church or club members, customers, or whatever. Chances are those expectations are behavioral in nature and include being friendly and honest, showing respect, keeping promises and honoring commitments, being helpful and supportive, giving you the benefit of the doubt, assuming that your motives are good and that your mistakes are unintentional, and a host of other things – like many of the topics presented in this book.

Now comes "the $64,000 question" – one that a well-known, bald and mustachioed TV psychologist might ask if he was addressing this issue:
What gives you the right to expect those things from other people?

Hmmmm. Kind of interesting when you think about it ... when you put it that way. Where *do* we get off thinking that people should interact with us in certain ways? Is it a right of birth? No it's not! Being born really only entitles you to those rights that are granted and protected by the laws of the land. Is it a right of morality? Getting closer – but morality is a some-what ambiguous term with different meanings to different people. So, if expecting others to act in certain ways is not a right of birth or morality, what is it? It's a right of behavior ... YOUR BEHAVIOR! And it's not an entitlement – it's a right that must be earned. How do you earn it? By following that wise and timeless "Golden Rule" principle: *Do unto others as you would have them do unto you.* Or more precisely for purposes of this discussion, *Expect from others only what you are willing to do, yourself.*

Here's the hard reality: when it comes to expectations, you've got two paths you can follow ... two choices you can make. You can be a **role model** – setting the example for others to follow. Or, you can be a **hypocrite** – wanting from others what you're not willing to give in return.

Those are the ends of the continuum and there's no middle ground.
The choice is yours.

> *He teaches me to be good who does me good.*
>
> ~ Thomas Fuller ~

Squelch Any Skepticism

Choose to Be Positive

An employee complains that management hasn't corrected an air conditioning problem. Shortly thereafter, management has a brand new unit installed. The employees response: *It's about freakin' time!* A team member criticizes a coworker for never acknowledging others' good work. That coworker makes an effort to change and compliments the critic twice in one week. The critic's thought: *She must be up to something!* A spouse complains about never receiving flowers. So, one day out of the clear blue, "Mr. or Ms. Good Intentions" comes home with a huge bouquet of roses – only to hear: *Okay, what did you do wrong?*

All those are examples of something called **skepticism** – reacting with doubt or suspicion to someone doing the things we think they *should* be doing … criticizing people for meeting our expectations. Is skepticism natural? Somewhat! Is it illogical? Very much so! Can it be counterproductive? Absolutely! If not carefully controlled, it can literally squash an individual's or organization's efforts to do what's good, right, and desired.

There are many problems inherent to skepticism. Perhaps the biggest is that it fosters no-win environments. If people don't act in certain ways, they get criticized or belittled. If they make an effort to change and actually act the way others think they should, their motives are questioned. They're "damned if they do and damned if they don't." Ever felt that way yourself? It's a lousy feeling! You start to question, "Why bother?" And eventually, realizing that you can't win no matter what you do, you stop trying altogether. As a result, nothing changes … nothing gets better. To put it in contemporary terms, that sucks!

Reflect again on your role models for working right – people who are successful in their careers and their relationships with coworkers. How do these folks react when others do what they want and expect? Do they respond with words like *It's about time* or *I wonder what she's up to?* I doubt it! I'm betting they're more positive – that they're much more likely to say things like *Wonderful! ... Terrific! ... Thank You!* Why? Because they understand that the manner in which they respond to everything in life is purely and simply a matter of their own choosing. And they know that opting for skepticism is NOT how they meet the responsibility we all share of contributing to a positive and productive working environment.

So, if you ever find skepticism creeping into your thought patterns at work, stop, lighten up, and give your coworkers a little more benefit of the doubt. If a manager, colleague, direct report (or whoever) makes an effort to do something good, why be critical? You'll be much better off by giving them some positive feedback ... and then following their lead. When that happens, everyone wins – including YOU!

When Mr. Fulton showed off his new invention, the steamboat, skeptics were crowded on the banks of the river yelling,
   "It'll never start, it'll never start!"
But it did. It got going with a lot of cranking and groaning, and as it made its way down the river, the skeptics were quiet for a brief moment. Then they started shouting,
   "It'll never stop, it'll never stop!"

Stand for Safety

Contribute to a Physically and Emotionally Safe Workplace

Of all the responsibilities that come with working right, none (I repeat, NONE) is more important than following safety procedures. You can't possibly be successful at work unless you're totally committed to safe work practices.

When you examine them, you find that most safety rules and procedures are about common sense standards and behaviors. But, as I said earlier, not everyone is blessed with an adequate helping of common sense. People sometimes do dumb things and they need to be protected from themselves! That why rules and procedural directives are developed; that's why it's critical that you know those rules ... and that you follow them to the letter.

Safety rules and health standards exist to protect YOU and the people around you. They're for *your* benefit. And that's the precise reason why violating them is stupidity at its utmost. Unintentionally exposing yourself (and others) to danger and unnecessary risk is problematic. Knowingly doing it is criminal! No one has the right to do that. Fact is, everyone has the responsibility to do just the opposite. So, when it comes to safety, know the rules ... follow the rules ... protect everyone around you.

Understandably, most people think of "safe work practices" in the context of *physical* safety – protecting people from injury and bodily harm. And clearly that is of paramount importance. But physical safety is not the only type you're responsible for. If you're going to be truly successful – if you want to – you must focus on EMOTIONAL safety as well!

What is an emotionally safe environment? It's one where people can do their work, speak their minds, share their ideas, and be themselves – all without fear of being teased, criticized, or belittled. That's something that *everyone* is entitled to ... that's the type of workplace that *everyone* must help create and maintain.

Ever had one of your ideas brutally shot down at a meeting? Ever been the butt of jokes because of the way you speak? Ever been embarrassed or made to "feel small" by others on your team? Ever avoided asking questions out of fear of being treated like you're stupid or incompetent? If so, there's no need to ask how you felt. And there's no need to ask how you suppose others will feel if you ever do those same things to them – you already know.

Physical safety. Emotional safety. Both are important ... both are your responsibility ... both are critical components of working right.

Is your workplace "safer" because of what YOU do?

Manage Your Mistakes

Own, Admit to, Fix, and Learn from Your Errors

You don't need a wealth of working experience to know that STUFF HAPPENS! Nobody's perfect. And no matter how good you are (or *think* you are) – or how well-intended you may be – you're occasionally going to screw up on the job. It happens to all of us ... to the very best of us. As an extremely competent coworker once told me, "I thought I made a mistake once, but I was wrong!"

When you make a job-related mistake, you have five basic response options ... five different approaches you can take:

1. You can **ignore it** (*The "I Couldn't Care Less" Approach*)
2. You can **hide it** (*The Cover-Up Approach*)
3. You can **blame others** (*The Deflection Approach*)
4. You can **blame circumstances** (*The Excuses Approach*)
5. You can **admit** to it, **fix** it, and **learn** from it – accepting any appropriate consequences like an adult.

Care to guess what approach that last one is? It's *The RESPONSIBLE Approach!*

So, which of these five responses does common sense tell you is more likely to lead to job and career success? Which of them was the way YOU responded to the last mistake *you* made? Which would you pass along to a child as good character-building advice?

Quest for Quality

Cut Complacency, Not Corners

"That's good enough!" Now there's a phrase we're all familiar with – one you've probably used more than once throughout your lifetime. I know I have. So here's an interesting question that's a lot more important to your job success than you might think: *When is good enough just that ... when is good really enough?*

A few people would argue that "good enough" is *never* enough ... that the job isn't done until it's perfect – which sounds great in theory, but isn't realistic in actual practice. Perfection is a great target to aim for as long as you accept the fact that you can't possibly hit it all the time.

Then, there are the folks on the opposite end of the continuum. Look at their behavior and it's clear that good enough is reached when they get bored or tired with the task at hand, when their shift is about to end, or when they feel the need to rationalize "cutting corners" – the telltale sign of complacent ("just get by") attitudes. Here's an example ...

Quite a while back I was helping one of my daughters with a high-school paper. After reviewing, editing, and revising the work a few times, she said it: *That's good enough!* I though for a moment and then asked, *Good enough for what?* Her reply: *Good enough to pass!* I followed with a query that she still remembers to this day – one that she used for motivation in her later college years:

> *So that's your goal ... just to pass? Aren't you selling yourself and your abilities short? Aren't you better than that?*

Okay. So, what's *your* answer? When is your work good enough? Here's my view: "Good enough" is reached only …

- When the job is completely done;
- When you've honored your (and your organization's) promises, commitments, and guarantees;
- When you've done the absolute best you can do;
- When extra effort will add no measurable value;
- When you've delivered the quality of goods or services that you expect from others when you're on the receiving end.

Anything short of those isn't *good*, isn't *enough*, and isn't meeting the responsibilities that accompany your paycheck. More importantly, anything short of those is selling *yourself* short.

Aren't YOU better than that?

If a man is called to be a
streetsweeper,
he should sweep streets
even as Michelangelo painted,
or Beethoven composed music,
or Shakespeare wrote poetry.

He should sweep streets so well
that all the hosts of heaven
and earth will pause to say,
here lived a great streetsweeper
who did his job well.

~ Martin Luther King Jr. ~

Savor Successes

Be a Cheerleader for Positive Contributions

One of the many things that top-notch workers seem to have in common is a true appreciation for achievement – theirs *and* others'. They *get* that when one member of the team is successful, everybody wins. They *understand* that recognizing accomplishments is one of the best ways to motivate themselves, and their coworkers, to keep pursuing them. They *know* that – in tough times like these – success is something to be enjoyed, celebrated, and encouraged. They *are* cheerleaders for positive contributions. And, with the exception of those who don't make the squad, most everyone likes cheerleaders.

Self-reflection time, again ...

Think of the last time you accomplished something good at work. How did you react? Did you pat yourself on the back, enjoy the moment, and share your happiness with others (without overly bragging)? If you did, GREAT! You deserved those good feelings. If you didn't, I've got just four words for you: WHY THE HECK NOT? Now, think about the last time a coworker did something fantastic. Did you pat that person on the back, encourage him or her to enjoy the moment, and share in their happiness? Depending on your answer, my responses are the same as those above: GREAT ... or WHY THE HECK NOT?!

Looking to be known as an indispensable team member who works right? Be happy when you and your teammates succeed ... and *show* it! When it comes to this topic, we'd all be wise to take a lesson from that classic childhood verse:

If you're happy and you know it, CLAP YOUR HANDS!

Embrace and Embody Ethics

Do What's Right

There's a dangerous balance occurring more and more in the corporate world, and it's scary! It seems as though for every organization or individual receiving an ethics award, there's another being charged with some type of impropriety. And this has led more than a few to conclude that we're right in the middle of an ethics and integrity crisis – in business, in politics, and as a society.

So what's all the hubbub about? What exactly is ETHICS, anyway? Well, if you turn to a dictionary for help, you find definitions such as: "a system of moral principles or values; the rules or standards governing the conduct of the members of a profession; accepted principles of right and wrong." Translated into simple, behavioral terms, it means doing what's good, fair, honest, and of course – legal.

Our grandparents, and generations before them, would probably be both amused and disturbed by the fact that we now create departments, appoint monitoring staff, and even write books – all to make sure we do what they knew as the *only* way to do business ... **the natural way to behave.** But then, they probably didn't face the same intense workplace and career pressures that lead to temptations of stretching the truth, trading quality for expediency, operating by exploiting "loopholes," and targeting the short-term, end-justifies-the-means, fast buck.

The good news is that most businesses (and most people that work in them) are doing right, fair, honest, and legal things every day. And that's how it needs to be – that's where YOU need to be – because the risks are way too great for doing otherwise. The reality is ...

■ **Your reputation** (yours and your organization's) **is at stake.** In the business world, reputation is everything. Your success hinges on it. Why? Because customers have choices. They research and compare vendors. And they do business with reputable organizations. Commit one ethical faux pas – which will overshadow scores of previous good actions – and you'll watch your customers go elsewhere. Not good!

■ **Your job is at stake.** If your business loses business, there's less of a need to keep you around. Whatever job security you may have had becomes nonexistent. And, with today's increased sensitivity and focus on business practices – combined with the need for organizations to protect themselves – ethics violations can result in job loss and legal prosecution. *Definitely* not good! That's precisely why you should care about ethics; that's precisely why you need to be a role model for doing what's right.

Here's the big code-breaker you need to remember: Whether or not you have an ethics department, or compliance officers, or a "code of conduct," the ethical makeup of your business begins and ends with YOU ... and all the other "you's" with whom you work. The actions you take, the decisions you make, and the daily behaviors you exhibit – whether noteworthy or seemingly insignificant – are ultimately how you and your organization will be judged. When it comes to ethics ...

Everyone is responsible! Everything counts!

COMMON RATIONALIZATIONS FOR NOT DOING WHAT'S RIGHT ... *TO AVOID*

"Everyone else does it!"
"They'll never miss it!"
"Nobody will care!"
"The boss does it!"
"No one will know!"
"I don't have time to do it right!"
"It's not all that important!"
"Some rules were meant to be broken!"
"It's not my job!"

ETHICAL ACTION CRITERIA

You can be confident that you're doing what's right if ...

- It's legal.

- It complies with established rules and guidelines.

- It's in sync with your organization's values.

- You're comfortable and guilt-free doing it.

- It matches your business's commitments and guarantees.

- You'd do it to your family and friends.

- You'd be perfectly okay with someone doing it to you.

- The most ethical person you know would do it.

MASTERING
"THE 3 R's"

Results

Some of us will do our jobs well and some will not, but
we will all be judged by just one thing – the RESULT.

~ Vince Lombardi ~

Coddle Your Customers

Make Excellent Service Your Top Priority

Ever stop to really think about what business you're in? Ask people, and they'll typically say things like: manufacturing, sales, healthcare, banking, government, computer software, education, retail, hospitality, etc. If those are the kind of answers you would give, you'd be only half right!

Here's a one-question test that you should be able to ace: If all of your customers went away, would your organization be able to stay afloat ... would you still have a job? Of course not! Well, that's your clue to the other half – arguably the more important half – of what you do: **YOU'RE IN THE CUSTOMER SERVICE BUSINESS.** So, in order to be successful, you not only need to be good at fixing equipment, writing programs, conducting tests, handling transactions, etc., you also need to be good at serving customers. Those who ignore this fact of working life run the risk of being thrust into *new* "careers": checking want ads, collecting meager unemployment (if they qualify), and trying to beat the odds on the few lotto tickets they can afford to buy. Now there's an impressive resume!

You see, it works like this: When you accepted employment with your organization, you took on a significant responsibility: taking care of the people who keep your business IN business. No job is any more important than that; no function is more closely linked to your organization's mission and its overall success. Like it or not, you have some heavy weight on your shoulders. We all do! It comes with the job. And, it's what gives us the opportunity to excel, stand out, and "shine."

Imagine for a moment that someone came to you and said, "Periodically, I'm going to give you some of my money." And that's exactly what he or she did. Wouldn't you appreciate that person? Wouldn't you bend over backwards to please ("coddle") them? Wouldn't you be happy, and cheerful, and grateful? Would he or she be your new BFF? You bet! Well, that's what customers do – they come in and give you money. And in doing so, they deserve the very best attentive, courteous, and quality service you can possibly deliver.

Is that what YOU do? If so, *way* to go … you're working right!

If it's not what you do, why isn't it?

It's not the employer who pays the wages.
Employers only handle the money.
It's the customer who pays the wages.

~ Henry Ford ~

Go with Great Goals

Plan Your Work, Work Your Plan, and Aim High

One of my lasting role models is a woman I used to work with. Her name was (still is) Kathy. She was younger than me, she had less business experience than me, and, in many ways, she was *wiser* than me. Kathy was successful in pretty much everything she did – from her health and family life, to her education and career. And she was dynamite at work. Her secret? Actually she had two. *First,* she had goals for everything – whether it was a short-term project she was working on, or a long-term dream she was pursuing. Her goals were big, action-driven, and success-oriented. She used to say (probably still does): "The higher you aim, the higher you hit!" And hit high she usually did. Why? Because of her *second* secret: she had plans, committed to them, adjusted them as necessary, and made them happen. There were daily "to do" lists, project timelines, family schedules, and career paths. She planned her work and worked her plan. And the results spoke for themselves. During the time we worked together, she was promoted twice, earned her MBA, and eventually left to start her own highly-successful business. I think of her often – especially when I'm tempted to settle for talent-squandering goals like *staying under the radar and just making it through the week.*

Do you have goals for your job ... your career? Is your aim high? Do you have plans for achieving the results you want and need? Hopefully you do! And if that's the case, three things are undoubtedly true:

1. You've mastered a key element of working right;
2. Success is in your present ... and your future;
3. You qualify to be someone else's role model ... someone else's "Kathy"!

Sweat the Small Stuff

Focus on Small, Incremental Improvements. Pay Attention to Details.

On the previous page I talked about the importance of having big ("great") goals. But here's the kicker – and it's something my friend Kathy understood, believed, and practiced:

The best way to achieve BIG goals is through SMALL actions!

You have to focus on the little things ... you have to sweat the small stuff. And the key word there is "sweat." Ya gotta work at it!

Don't waste time looking for gigantic things to tackle that will take you quickly and directly to your desired end state. They don't exist in the real world! Think about it. There's really no one big thing you can do that will make you a great parent. There's no one-time gesture that will make you the perfect friend. And there's no single action you can take that will set your career and give you lasting success at work.

Bottom line: There's no Scotty to beam you to where you want to be. The only way to get there is through a bunch of things ... a bunch of steps taken one at a time. Large successes are sum totals – the result of multiple little successes added together. As the late vaudevillian Eddie Cantor once said:

"It takes twenty years to become an overnight success."

Remember those words – they're equally applicable to your life, your career, and your current job.

When you break employment down to its most basic level, you see that jobs (yours and mine) exist for one primary purpose: **to produce results.** Combine that with the fact that very few of us are ever in the driver's seat for big projects or major decisions, and it's clear that most people's results come from small, daily actions. Our changes evolve. Our improvements are incremental. Our successes are built over time. And they all involve DETAILS!

Think of it this way: Desired end states like top-notch quality, superior service, satisfying relationships, job successes, and rewarding careers all have something in common – they're all jigsaw puzzles. The only way you get to the desired ("big") picture is by assembling a bunch of little pieces that interlock. Each of those pieces is equally important ... each requires attention and focus. Ignore one or more of them, and the picture is never complete. Well, those little puzzle pieces represent *everything* you do at work. From the things you say, to the activities you perform, to the attitudes you display, each action matters ... every detail counts.

Want to complete your job success puzzle? If so, here's a piece you'll need ...

Sweat
the
Small Stuff

A "Crash Course" on WORKING RIGHT

10 important words to say:
> *"What can I do to help YOU be more successful?"*

9 important words to say:
> *"You can count on me to do what's right."*

8 important words to say:
> *"That's my responsibility and I will do it."*

7 important words to say:
> *"I'd like to hear what you think."*

6 important words to say:
> *"Let's focus on solving the problem."*

5 important words to say:
> *"You did a great job!"*

4 important words to say:
> *"Let's all work together."*

3 important words to say:
> *"I respect you."*

2 important words to say:
> *"Thank you."*

The **1** important word to say:
> ***"WE"***

Share Your Skills

Pass Along What You Know and Do Well to Help Others Succeed

Let's play fortune teller for a few seconds. You be the "seer." Who do you predict has the greatest chance of being successful at work (and in life) – a giver or a taker ... someone who shares or someone who hoards ... a person who helps others or one who's mostly out for himself or herself? Well, Zoltar, how'd you do? I'm guessing you selected the former in each example. If so, you're good, you're right, and you need to remember your own predictions! (BTW: If you picked any of the latters, it's time to turn in the turban.)

One of the truly great things about being human is that each of us has our own set of special talents, skills, and abilities. We're all blessed with certain gifts – things we know and do really well. But along with those gifts comes the need to decide how we'll use them. And in determining that, we all face the same two choices: 1) Use our strengths exclusively for *our* personal benefit, or 2) Share them with others who may be lacking in one or more skills that we take for granted. In other words, we can "look out for number one" or we can "pay it forward." You don't have to be a Zoltar to know which of those choices is best!

Questions to Answer

1. What are my special skills and abilities ... what am I good at?
2. Which of my coworkers could benefit from my areas of strength?
3. What specifically can/will I do to share what I know?
4. What strengths will I ask each of my coworkers to share with me?

Cherish
Constructive Criticism

Use Feedback to Improve Your Performance and Results

> ### Instruction to Reader
> If you are a results-producing machine who is as good as it gets, knows everything there is to know, and can't possibly improve in any way, proceed directly to page 52.

Still here? Of course you are! Me too! With the exception of a few egomaniacs and misguided souls who might actually *have* jumped ahead to the next section, we all realize that nobody's perfect. People make mistakes. There's always more we can (and need to) learn. And, no matter how good we are, we can do even better ... **we all can improve the results we produce and the success that comes with them.** YOU can do that – but you'll need two things ...

First, you need the DESIRE to improve and enjoy increased success. The reason for that is obvious: without motivation there is no action. No need to talk about that anymore. I'll just assume you already have the desire – otherwise you probably would have closed this book long before reaching this page. Good for you!

Second, you need FEEDBACK ... you need constructive criticism. Why? Because, in order to address your improvement opportunities, you have to know what they *are*! But, like everyone else, you have "blind spots." You don't always have an accurate read on how well (or not so well) you're doing. So, you have to rely on others – your boss, your coworkers, and your customers.

To be sure, the need for feedback from others makes perfect sense both logically and academically. But let's get *really* real. Nobody likes to be criticized – including YOU! Sometimes you know bad news is coming, many times you're caught off guard, and, just about always, it's a jolt to your self-esteem. As a result, the tendency is to receive it with more defensiveness than receptivity. But you've got to get over that ... you've got to get past it ... you need to tweak your perspective. As long as the criticism is *constructive* in nature, you should accept it for what it is: A GIFT! You're getting information about how you can be more successful. And that's something for which you truly should be grateful.

If you happen to work in an organization where feedback is frequently provided to you, great! You're fortunate. Pay attention to what you hear and **ACT on the information**. If you're like most folks, however, you'll need more performance evaluation data than is given to you. That means you'll have to ASK for it. Make a habit of posing the *How am I doing?* question to someone at least once a month. Solicit information from your manager, a trusted coworker, or a customer you're serving. To pinpoint specific areas to work on, try asking:

> *What one or two things can I do to be more successful?*
> *What can I do to serve you better in the future?*

And when you get an answer, be sure to thank the person ... for helping you WORK RIGHT!

Conquer Conflicts

Don't Let Problems Fester

Either it has already happened or it's waiting down the road. Count on it. Expect it. Sooner or later, you're going to find yourself involved in a conflict (a.k.a. having a "beef") with someone at work. Maybe the person will offend or otherwise "wrong" you in some way. Perhaps you'll feel that he or she has inappropriately interfered with your plans and activities. Or it could be that a difference of opinion about a work-related issue has grown into a strong and emotionally-charged disagreement. Regardless of the nature of the conflict, it's likely that your focus will be interrupted, your stomach will churn, and your ability to do your very best work will be hampered. It will "stick in your craw" – negatively affecting your attitude, your performance, and your results. Something will need to be done. And that something is NOT merely living with the problem and hoping it will resolve itself over time.

Here's one more you can take to the bank: Unlike fine wine, conflicts that are left alone rarely improve with age. They're much more likely to fester and decay. Sure, you can ignore them, or try to live with them, but the odds are miniscule that they'll evaporate into thin air and then all will be well with the world, again. Fact is, conflicts must be resolved the same way they were started in the first place – though human actions. They must be confronted, addressed, and worked through. **Ya gotta talk it out!**

Will doing so be easy and pleasant? *Probably* not! Very few people are comfortable with the thought of talking to others about mutual problems. Is that a good enough reason for avoiding issues? *Absolutely* not! When it comes to conflict, time heals all wounds – as long as they are *treated* first.

Tips for
Effective Conflict-Resolution Discussions

Have a walk-in strategy. Plan what you'll say and do BEFORE you meet. Think of the exact words you'll use to open the conversation – and practice them.

Get to the point. Don't allow the issue to become clouded with excessive small talk. You can be respectful, polite, and tactful – and still be DIRECT.

Attack the problem, not the person. Stay focused on what actually occurred. Avoid accusations or assigning blame. Minimize the use of the word "you" when starting the discussion.

Share your feelings ... and how you're impacted. Use "I" statements to describe how what happened has made you feel and how it has affected you. Example: *When that happened, I really felt belittled, embarrassed, and under-appreciated.*

Pay attention to your body language. Avoid negative "message-sending gestures" such as arm crossing, finger tapping, head shaking, and eye rolling.

Control your emotions. Expect the unexpected. Assume – going into the discussion – that something may happen to trigger your emotions, and have a plan for exactly what you'll do to avoid "losing it."

Think "dialog" – not "monolog." Remember that effective communication is a two-way street. Be sure to concentrate as much on *hearing* as you do on making sure you're heard.

Focus on Fixes

Offer Solutions Instead of Lamenting Over Problems

Around my house, I'm known by several nicknames. One of the more flattering ones is "Mr. Fix-It." I've been blessed with a knack for repairing things that are broken, tweaking things that aren't running right, and replacing things that have gone kaput. Knowing that, my family tends to bring all of their repair-related problems to me – including minor things that they *could* handle themselves.

Most of the time, I like being the one my family relies on; I like being the "hero" who solves the problem and saves the day. Occasionally, however, I find myself overwhelmed with an overflowing list of repair to-do's. The fuel gauge on my coping mechanism is reading "empty." And when my wife or kids march up to inform me of yet another thing they want me to handle, I get testy and say: *So, what have you done about it ... besides telling me? It sure would be nice if you'd at least try to fix a few things on your own before dropping them on me!*

Yep, I've said that at home. And I admit it, I've also said it at work – to team members who somehow felt that the totality of their problem-solving responsibilities were lamenting and telling the boss, period. Those employees didn't get it! No surprise – they were *not* the most successful people I've ever managed or worked with.

So, what's the lesson here ... what's the key learning? Is it: Don't point out problems or bring bad news to the boss? Not at all! People need to know when things are going south. But working right involves more than just being a messenger. You also must do whatever you can to be a "fixer."

Fixers rarely waste time "celebrating" problems. They're more interested in finding and implementing solutions. They have a distinctive vocabulary that makes them easy to spot. After describing problems, they say things like:

... and here's what I've done about it!

or

... and here's how I think we can correct it!

or

... I'm not sure how to fix it. But if you can give me a little direction, I'd like to tackle it!

Trust me, managers *really* appreciate team members who offer solutions as well as problems – or who demonstrate a willingness to attempt the fix with a little guidance. Wouldn't you?

So, the next time you come face to face with a problem at work, try doing something about it. Instead of complaining, or commiserating, or handing it off to others, make an effort to fix it. If you do …

You *will* produce more results,
You *will* be more successful,
You *will* be WORKING RIGHT!

If you're not part of the solution, you ARE part of the problem!

Leave a Lasting Legacy

Make a Positive Difference

You're just about at the end of this book, almost all of the "lessons" have been presented, and now it's time for the final exam. It's one item – multiple choice. I guarantee you'll pass. Here it is:

> Successful employees are those who:
> a. Make a positive difference where they work
> b. Make no difference at all where they work
> c. Make a negative difference where they work

No rocket science there. Obviously the correct answer is (a.) – "Make a positive difference where they work." These are the people we want to be around and work next to. They impact us in the best possible way. They are doers, achievers, and contributors who leave things much better than they find them. Service is better, quality is higher, results are greater, and things run more smoothly *because* they are involved. This is the group you'll want to be part of ... and stay part of.

To be sure, some people are members of the (b.) group – individuals who "make no difference at all where they work." These folks deserve our pity. The contribute little to nothing, they take up space, they use up air, and they squander the skills and talents they have been blessed with. They make no mark ... they leave no legacy. What a waste! What a shame! What a group to avoid!

Fortunately, the (c.) group – those who "make a negative difference where they work" – is very small in size. And their employment often doesn't last very long. But while they are working, they can do some serious damage through caustic attitudes and counterproductive behaviors. They deserve our disdain, not our pity. Our pity goes out to everyone else – the people they work with and for. But this little group does serve a purpose. They show us what NOT to do. Learn from them … at a distance!

Now it's true confessions time. I admit it. I fibbed a little. There actually are TWO items/questions in your final exam. Here's the second one – which undoubtedly will require more thought than the first:

> My coworkers and customers would probably say that I:
> a. Make a positive difference at work
> b. Make no difference at all at work
> c. Make a negative difference at work

Hmmmm … not so easy! If you answered (b.), I recommend you reread this book a bunch more times. If you answered (c.), my best advice is to start dusting off your resume. But hopefully you selected (a.). And if that's the case, think about *why* you chose that answer. What have you done in the past – and what are you currently doing – to make a positive difference? What behaviors would you cite as evidence that your team and your organization are better because of you? Most importantly, what can (and will) you do tomorrow, and the next day, and the next, to WORK RIGHT and build a lasting legacy?

Final exam finished? Nope … it's just begun!

DO I WORK RIGHT? A Self-Assessment

Read the statements below. Think about each one, and then respond as honestly as possible.

YES NO

[Y] [N] 1. I am a good listener. I make a conscious effort to hear and understand the ideas and concerns of my coworkers and customers.

[Y] [N] 2. I value and appreciate people with ideas, backgrounds, and demographic characteristics that are different from mine.

[Y] [N] 3. I am a considerate person. I place great importance on being polite and respectful. I focus on others' needs as well as my own.

[Y] [N] 4. I try my very best to always DO my very best. My attitude, behaviors, and the quality of my work reflect someone with self-respect.

[Y] [N] 5. I understand our organization's mission, I believe in it, and I'm committed to doing my part to make it happen.

[Y] [N] 6. I share the spotlight. Whenever I'm praised, I mention and thank the coworkers who contributed to my success.

[Y] [N] 7. I avoid wasting or misusing organizational resources of all types. I take only what I need for business purposes – and use it to its fullest.

[Y] [N] 8. I regularly display empathy in my dealings at work. I avoid judging others and make a sincere effort to see things from their perspectives.

[Y] [N] 9. I meet all of the responsibilities that come with my job. My coworkers can always count on me to carry my share of the load.

[Y] [N] 10. I avoid hypocrisy with a passion. I never ask coworkers to do what I'm not willing to do myself. I model the behaviors I expect from others.

[Y] [N] 11. I make a special effort to avoid being skeptical. I give others the benefit of the doubt and I work at viewing situations optimistically.

[Y] [N] 12. I follow all safety rules and procedures to the letter. And I avoid behaviors that might jeopardize the *emotional* safety of my work group.

[Y] [N] 13. When I make a mistake, I admit it, I fix it, and I learn from it. I never blame others for my errors.

[Y] [N] 14. I am totally committed to quality. I make a conscious effort to do my best work with every task I perform. You rarely hear me say, "That's good enough!"

Y N 15. I appreciate and celebrate successes – mine and my teammates'. I'm happy for my coworkers when they do well … and I let them know.

Y N 16. It's critically important for me to perform with ethics and integrity – even if others don't. You can always count on me to do what's right.

Y N 17. I am committed to providing the best customer service possible. I understand that serving customers is why my job exists. I always go "the extra mile" for the people I serve.

Y N 18. I maintain lofty goals for myself and my teammates, and I work hard to achieve them. I plan my work and I work my plans. I aim high.

Y N 19. I pay attention to details and focus on making many small, continuous improvements. I understand that big goals are achieved through lots of little actions – and that *everything* I do matters.

Y N 20. I regularly share my knowledge, skills, and talents with others to help them succeed and grow. I pass along the gifts I have been given.

Y N 21. I appreciate constructive criticism. I ask for it, I accept it, I pay attention to it, and I use it to improve my performance and results.

Y N 22. Whenever I have a conflict with a coworker, I make an effort to resolve the issue in a mutually beneficial way – rather than ignoring it and letting it fester.

Y N 23. I'm a "fixer." Whenever I face problems at work, I try to resolve or identify possible solutions *before* telling others about them.

Y N 24. I care deeply about the reputation I am building and the legacy I am leaving at work. I can honestly say that I'm committed to making a positive difference for my teammates, my customers, and my organization in everything I do. This place is better because I am here.

Now, go back and highlight each of the statements for which you checked the NO box (there should be some … unless, of course, you're perfect). These are the areas you should work on in order to increase your individual effectiveness and overall job success. Develop informal action plans, make a personal commitment to see them through, and get started. And for all those that you checked YES: Congratulations … and keep doing what you're doing!

CLOSING THOUGHTS

I leave you with this last bit of straight scoop: Whether you're an experienced worker or someone just starting employment, no matter if this is your ideal position or merely one stop on a larger career journey, you need to be successful. Why? Because your future is at stake! **What you do *today* determines where you'll be – and what you'll enjoy – *tomorrow.*** Remember those words. Repeat them if you ever find yourself slacking off and thinking "this is just a job." You see, my friend, it's much more than a job – it's your life! Those who get that, get ahead; those who don't get it, get much less than their true potential could bring them.

One of the best things about job success is that it's not all that hard to achieve. Anyone can do it … it's there for the taking. You just need to practice **"The 3 R's"**:

Show RESPECT for …

Your coworkers … Your customers … Your organization
and its resources … YOURSELF!

Take RESPONSIBILITY for …

Carrying your share of the load … Having a positive attitude …

Helping others succeed … DOING WHAT'S RIGHT!

Produce RESULTS by …

Adding value through everything you do … Honoring your part
of the organization's mission … Making a positive difference …

LEAVING A LASTING LEGACY!

Think for a moment. Ask yourself …

Do I try to give my best effort in everything I do?

Do I complain or do I contribute?

Am I a team player who helps others succeed?

Am I responsible? Dependable? A person of integrity?

Those are the qualities of people who succeed in good times and in bad. And they're critical for your job, your career, and your future. Ignore them and watch those who are focused on success zoom past you. Embrace them and YOU WIN!

The choice is yours. Choose well. Choose to

WORK RIGHT.

Success in business

requires training and discipline

and hard work.

But if you're not frightened

by these things, the

opportunities are just as great

today as they ever were.

~ David Rockefeller ~

THE AUTHOR

STEVE VENTURA is a recognized and respected author, educator, book producer, and award-winning training program designer. His work reflects over 30 years of human resource development experience – both as a practitioner and a business consultant.

His WalkTheTalk.com books include:
- *Walk Awhile in My Shoes*
- *Five Star Teamwork*
- *What To Do When Conflict Happens*
- *Walk The Talk Gift Book*

And the "Right Stuff" book series which includes:
- *Start Right, Stay Right*
- *Lead Right*
- *Serve Right*
- *Work Right*

THE PUBLISHER

For over 30 years, *WalkTheTalk.com* has been dedicated to one simple goal...one single mission: *To provide you and your organization with high-impact resources for your personal and professional success.*

Walk The Talk resources are designed to:

- Develop your skills and confidence
- Inspire your team
- Create customer enthusiasm
- Build leadership skills
- Stretch your mind
- Handle tough "people problems"
- Develop a culture of respect and responsibility
- And, most importantly, help you achieve your personal and professional goals.

**Contact the Walk The Talk team at
1.888.822.9255
or visit us at *www.walkthetalk.com.***

Visit

WALKTHETALK.COM
Resources for Personal and Professional Success

To Learn More

Leadership and Employee Development Centre

- Develop your Leaders
- Build Employee Commitment
- Achieve Business Results

NEW Walk The Talk Digital Resources on Demand

- Immediately access information
- Over 50 "how-to" topics
- Fast and user-friendly

Motivational Gift Books

- Inspire your Team
- Create Customer Enthusiasm
- Reinforce Core Values

Free Newsletters

To Include:
The Leadership Solution
Weekly tips to help you and your
colleagues become more effective
and respectful leaders.